May the light of Christ continue to shine
in your heart for all the world to see.

To: _____

From: _____

On this Day: _____

GIFTS FROM OUR FATHER
A Catholic Prayer Book for Kids

Ever Ancient, Ever New.

Written and Curated by Tom Wall

Illustrated by Martin Whitmore

Layout by Ron Tupper

Aquinas Ventures, LLC
Green Bay, Wisconsin 54305

Nihil Obstat
Reverend James P. Massart, D. Min., Ph.D.

Imprimatur
The Most Reverend David L. Ricken, DD, JCL
Bishop of Green Bay

Green Bay, Wisconsin   USA

December 11, 2014

The *Nihil Obstat* and *Imprimatur* are official declarations that a book is considered to be free of doctrinal or moral error.
It is not implied that those who have granted the *Nihil Obstat* or *Imprimatur*
agree with the contents, opinions, or statements expressed.

In memory of...

my Grandma Sophie, who not only believed in God's Word,
but truly lived it by the way she loved and served others.

Dedicated to...

all those who desire to know God, grow in their faith, and share it with the ones they love.

May everyone who comes to know us, know *who* we are and *whose* we are by the way we live our lives.

With Gratitude to...

my family, friends, teachers, priests, sisters, and Kickstarter backers... thank you.
Without your prayers, guidance, and support, this book would never have been possible.

Marty and Ron... God blessed you with many incredible gifts. Thank you for graciously sharing them in this book.

We are all companions on the journey. Thank you for being a part of mine. - Tom

When you pray, what do you talk to God about?

There are four forms of prayer.

GRATITUDE (Thank You!) – We pray to thank God for all of the blessings in our lives.

PETITION (Help!) – We pray to ask God to help us with the challenges that we face.

FORGIVENESS (Oops!) – We pray to tell God we're sorry and to ask Him to forgive us.

ADORATION (Wow!) – We pray to honor God for all that He is and all that He does.

Every day, it's important that we make time
to find a quiet place to talk to God.

Let us pray.

Pray as though everything depended on God.
Work as though everything depended on you. – *St. Augustine*

Did you know?

The word 'Catholic' means 'Universal'.

Every day, Catholics from all over the world gather at Mass
and recite the same prayers, listen to the same Gospel, and receive Holy Communion.

Although we live in different countries and speak different languages,
we remain one in our faith and our beliefs. Together, we are Catholic.

Nicene Creed

I believe in one God,
the Father almighty,
maker of heaven and earth,
of all things visible and invisible.

I believe in one Lord Jesus Christ,
the Only Begotten Son of God,
born of the Father before all ages.
God from God, Light from Light,
true God from true God,
begotten, not made, consubstantial with the Father;
through him all things were made.
For us men and for our salvation
he came down from heaven,
and by the Holy Spirit was incarnate of the Virgin Mary,
and became man.

For our sake he was crucified under Pontius Pilate,
he suffered death and was buried,
and rose again on the third day
in accordance with the Scriptures.
He ascended into heaven
and is seated at the right hand of the Father.
He will come again in glory
to judge the living and the dead
and his kingdom will have no end.

I believe in the Holy Spirit, the Lord, the giver of life,
who proceeds from the Father and the Son,
who with the Father and the Son is adored and glorified,
who has spoken through the prophets.

I believe in one, holy, catholic and apostolic Church.
I confess one Baptism for the forgiveness of sins
and I look forward to the resurrection of the dead
and the life of the world to come. Amen.

Did you know?

No other organization...

IT'S GOOD TO BE CATHOLIC!

feeds more people,

houses more people,

clothes more people,

educates more people,

visits more imprisoned people,

and **provides healthcare** to more people

than the Catholic Church.

DOING GOD'S WORK...

We are called to serve others.
We are called to be Christ to and for one another.

How will you live your Catholic faith?

7 Corporal Works of Mercy

- Feed the hungry.
- Give drink to the thirsty.
- Clothe the naked.
- Shelter the homeless.
- Visit the sick.
- Visit those imprisoned.
- Bury the dead.

7 Spiritual Works of Mercy

- Teach the ignorant.
- Counsel the doubtful.
- Admonish sinners.
- Bear wrongs patiently.
- Forgive offenses willingly.
- Comfort the afflicted.
- Pray for the living and the dead.

Spread love wherever you go. — *Bl. Mother Teresa*

HABEMUS PAPAM!

You are Peter, and upon this rock I will build my church...
I will give you the keys to the kingdom of heaven.
Matthew 16: 18, 19 (NRSV)

On March 13, 2013, Cardinal Jorge Mario Bergoglio of Argentina was elected the 266th Pope. Before being introduced on the balcony of St. Peter's Square, Cardinal Bergoglio chose the name Francis, after St. Francis of Assisi. Pope Francis is the first Pope from the Americas, and is also the first Jesuit Pope.

Prayer for Our Holy Father

Lord Jesus Christ,
We ask Your abundant blessings
on our spiritual leader, Pope Francis.
Send Your Holy Spirit upon him
that he may be a brother to all
of his faithful and a true servant to Almighty God.

Strengthen him daily to complete the immense duties
of the Church with grace and compassion.
Allow him to be a humble leader
who strives to bring peace, justice and truth into our world.

Above all, bestow upon our Holy Father
Your gifts of faith, hope and love
so that he unceasingly proclaims your Holy Name.
Mother Mary and all the holy angels and saints of God,
we ask you to guide Pope Francis this day and always. Amen.

Anybody can be Pope; the proof of this is that I have become one. – *St. John XXIII*

THE HOLY TRINITY

The Holy Trinity is one God in three persons.

God the Father created us.
God the Son came to live among us.
God the Holy Spirit abides with us.

The Solemnity of the Most Holy Trinity (Trinity Sunday)
is celebrated on the first Sunday after Pentecost.

We begin and end our prayers by calling upon the Holy Trinity as we bless ourselves with the Sign of the Cross.

The Sign of the Cross

In the name of the Father,
and of the Son,
and of the Holy Spirit. Amen.

Act of Faith

O my God,
I firmly believe that you are one God in three divine persons,
Father, Son and Holy Spirit.
I believe that your divine Son became man and died for our sins,
and that he will come to judge the living and the dead.
I believe these and all the truths which the Holy Catholic Church teaches,
because in revealing them you can neither deceive nor be deceived.

Act of Hope

O my God,
relying on Your almighty power and infinite mercy and promises,
I hope to obtain pardon of my sins,
the help of Your grace and life everlasting,
through the merits of Jesus Christ,
my Lord and Redeemer. Amen.

And now faith, hope, and love abide, these three; and the greatest of these is love.
1 Corinthians 13: 13 (NRSV)

Act of Love

O my God,
I love you above all things,
with my whole heart and soul,
because you are all good and worthy of all my love.
I love my neighbor as myself for the love of you.
I forgive all who have injured me and I ask pardon of all whom I have injured.

Act of Contrition

O my God,
I am heartily sorry for having offended you.
I detest all my sins because of your punishments.
But most of all because they offend you, my God,
who are all good and deserving of all my love.
I firmly resolve, with the help of your grace,
to sin no more and to avoid the near occasions of sin. Amen.

The sign of sincere love is to forgive wrongs done to us.
It was with such love that the Lord loved the world. – *St. Mark the Ascetic*

THE LITURGICAL CALENDAR

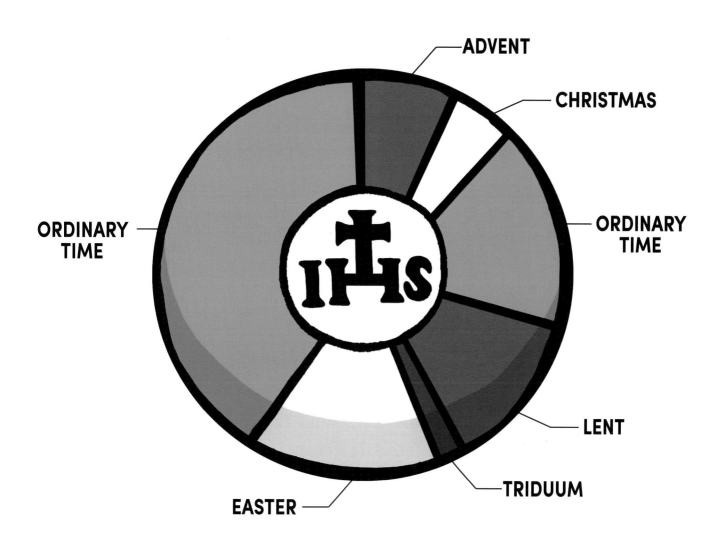

ADVENT

CHRISTMAS

ORDINARY TIME

ORDINARY TIME

LENT

TRIDUUM

EASTER

Did you know?

There are certain days of the year we are required to attend Mass. These days are called Holy Days of Obligation.

<u>Holy Days of Obligation in the United States</u>

Every Sunday (or Saturday after 4 p.m.)

Solemnity of Mary, Mother of God – January 1
(unless it falls on a Saturday or Monday)

Ascension of the Lord – 40 days after Easter Sunday
(Moved from Ascension Thursday to the following Sunday in most U.S. dioceses)

Assumption of Mary – August 15
(unless it falls on a Saturday or Monday)

All Saints' Day – November 1
(unless it falls on a Saturday or Monday)

Immaculate Conception – December 8

Christmas – December 25

ADVENT

The season of Advent is the four weeks before Christmas, and marks the beginning of the liturgical year. During Advent, we await and prepare our hearts for the birth of Jesus.

On each of the four Sundays of Advent, we light a new candle on the Advent wreath.

Advent Prayer

Father, in the wilderness of the Jordan
you sent a messenger to prepare people's hearts
for the coming of your Son.

Help me to hear his words and repent of my sins,
so that I may clearly see the way to walk,
the truth to speak,
and the life to live for Him,
our Lord Jesus Christ. Amen.

Look, the virgin shall conceive and bear a son, and they shall name him Emmanuel, which means "God is with us." *Matthew 1: 23 (NRSV)*

To you is born this day in the city of David a Savior, who is the Messiah, the Lord. *Luke 2:11 (NRSV)*

CHRISTMAS

We celebrate the birth of Jesus on December 25, the Nativity of Our Lord.

Birth or Adoption Prayer

My heart overflows with praise for you, God,
as I think of the blessing this child is to our family.
Guide me in my role as a parent.
Make me an instrument of your love.
Let me give myself unselfishly
so my child might know the joy and security
of being loved unconditionally.

Give me the wisdom to help my child
discover life's beauty and wonders
while nurturing our family's faith
in your abiding presence. Amen.

- Jeannie Hannemann

Prayer for the Dignity of Human Life

Lord and giver of all life,
help us to value each person,
created in love by you.

In your mercy, guide and assist our efforts
to promote the dignity and value of all human life,
born and unborn.

We ask this through Christ our Lord. Amen.

Out of darkness is born the light. – *St. Catherine of Siena*

When they had heard the king, they set out; and there, ahead of them, went the star that they had seen at its rising, until it stopped over the place where the child was. *Matthew 2:9 (NRSV)*

EPIPHANY

We celebrate the Epiphany, the day the Son of God was revealed to the world, on the Sunday between January 2 and January 8. This is the day when the three Magi traveled to meet and honor our newborn Savior with gifts of gold, frankincense, and myrrh.

Stewardship Prayer

Generous and loving God,
You call us to be disciples of your Son Jesus
and good stewards of all your many gifts.
Open our minds and hearts to a greater awareness
and deeper appreciation
of your countless blessings.
Transform us through the power of your Spirit
to nurture a Stewardship way of life
marked by faith-filled prayer,
service to our neighbor
and generous sharing.
Teach us to be faithful servants of your gifts.
With Mary's help, may we return ten-fold
the gifts entrusted to us.
We pray through Christ, our Lord. Amen.

- Catholic Diocese of Green Bay

Prayer for Generosity

Lord, teach me to be generous.
Teach me to serve you as you deserve;
to give and not to count the cost,
to fight and not to heed the wounds,
to toil and not to seek for rest,
to labor and not to ask for reward,
save that of knowing that I do your will.

- St. Ignatius of Loyola

From everyone to whom much has been given, much will be required; and from the one to whom much has been entrusted, even more will be demanded. *Luke 12:48 (NRSV)*

LENT

Lent is the 40-day period of renewal and reflection that is meant for us to focus on the life, death, and resurrection of Jesus.

During these forty days,
we are called to pray frequently,
give generously, and sacrifice freely.

Prayer for Lent

O God, bless us during this season of spiritual renewal.
Fill our minds and hearts with love,
that we may be a sign of Jesus to all those living in our midst.

Ash Wednesday is the first day
of the season of Lent.

HOLY WEEK

 Holy Week begins on Palm Sunday when Jesus enters the city of Jerusalem, and ends on Good Friday when He is crucified on Mount Calvary.

TRIDUUM

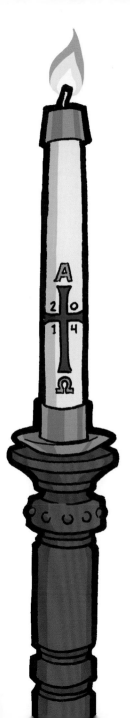

The Sacred Paschal Triduum is the three-day period during Holy Week that includes Holy Thursday, Good Friday, and the Easter Vigil.

HOLY THURSDAY

On the evening of Holy Thursday, we gather at Mass to relive the night Jesus washed the feet of His apostles and shared the Eucharist with them at The Last Supper.

GOOD FRIDAY

On the afternoon of Good Friday, we come together to venerate the cross and remember the day Jesus was crucified and died for our sins.

EASTER VIGIL

On the night of Holy Saturday, we gather to light the Easter candle, listen to the Word of God, share in the sacraments of Baptism, Confirmation, and Holy Communion, and rejoice in Jesus' resurrection from the dead.

THE STATIONS OF THE CROSS

1. Jesus is condemned to death.

2. Jesus carries His cross.

We adore You, O Christ, and we praise You.

**Because by Your holy cross,
You have redeemed the world.**

8. Jesus meets the women of Jerusalem.

9. Jesus falls the third time.

10. Jesus is stripped
of His clothes.

11. Jesus is nailed to the cross.

12. Jesus dies on the cross.

3. Jesus falls the first time.

4. Jesus meets His mother.

5. Simon of Cyrene helps Jesus carry the cross.

6. Veronica wipes the face of Jesus.

7. Jesus falls the second time.

13. Jesus is taken down from the cross.

14. Jesus is laid in the tomb.

Alleluia! He is Risen!

EASTER

Three days after Jesus was crucified, we celebrate the day He rose from the dead on Easter Sunday. The Resurrection of the Lord is the most important feast day of our liturgical year because it establishes that Jesus was truly the Son of God.

For God so loved the world
that he gave his only Son,
so that everyone who believes in him
may not perish but may have eternal life.

— John 3:16 (NRSV)

Do not abandon yourselves to despair. We are the Easter people and hallelujah is our song. – *St. John Paul II*

PENTECOST

Fifty days after Easter, we celebrate Pentecost. This is the day the Holy Spirit descended upon the apostles in the Upper Room.

Prayer to the Holy Spirit

Breathe in me, O Holy Spirit,
that my thoughts may all be holy.
Act in me, O Holy Spirit,
that my work, too, may be holy.
Draw my heart, O Holy Spirit,
that I love but what is holy.
Strengthen me, O Holy Spirit,
to defend all that is holy.
Guard me, then, O Holy Spirit,
that I always may be holy. Amen.

Confirmation Prayer

All-powerful God, Father of our Lord Jesus Christ,
by water and the Holy Spirit
you freed your sons and daughters from sin
and gave them new life.
Send your Holy Spirit upon them
to be their helper and guide.
Give them the spirit of wisdom and understanding,
the spirit of right judgment and courage,
the spirit of knowledge and reverence.
Fill them with the spirit of wonder and awe in your presence.
Through Christ our Lord.

-from Order of Confirmation

He saw the heavens torn apart and the Spirit descending like a dove on him. And a voice came from heaven, "You are my Son, the Beloved; with you I am well pleased." *Mark 1:10–11 (NRSV)*

SEVEN SACRAMENTS

The Seven Sacraments are sacred ceremonies at the heart of our lives as Catholics that were given to us by Jesus. Throughout our lifetime, we receive and participate in the Sacraments to welcome God's grace into our lives and come to know Him more fully.

BAPTISM

The soul is regenerated in the sacred waters of baptism and thus becomes God's child. - *St. Maximilian Kolbe*

FIRST RECONCILIATION

In failing to confess, Lord, I would only hide You from myself, not myself from You. – *St. Augustine*

FIRST COMMUNION

In one day the Eucharist will make you produce more for the glory of God than a whole lifetime without it. - *St. Peter Julian Eymard*

CONFIRMATION

Christ has no body now but mine. He prays in me, works in me, looks through my eyes, speaks through my words, works through my hands, walks with my feet and loves with my heart. – *St. Teresa of Avila*

MARRIAGE

There is no union so precious and so fruitful between husband and wife as that of holy devotion, in which they should mutually lead and sustain each other. – *St. Francis de Sales*

HOLY ORDERS

Lord, if your people need me, I will not refuse the work. Your will be done. – *St. Martin of Tours*

ANOINTING OF THE SICK

Let us touch the dying, the poor, the lonely and the unwanted according to the graces we have received and let us not be ashamed or slow to do the humble work. – *Bl. Mother Teresa*

THE MASS

The night before Jesus was crucified on the cross, He gathered with His twelve apostles in the Upper Room for the Last Supper. He consecrated the bread and wine and shared it with His followers as the Sacrifice of His Body and Blood.

Every time we gather together at Mass, we receive Communion to give thanks, to remember, and to relive the Last Supper and the Sacrifice that Jesus made for all of us.

"The Eucharist is **the source and summit** of the Christian life."
(Lumen Gentium, no. 11; cf. Catechism of the Catholic Church, no. 1324)

Jesus taught a new sacrifice that the Church received from the Apostles and offers throughout the whole world. – *St. Irenaeus*

LITURGY OF THE WORD

During the Liturgy of the Word, we focus on **listening** to God's Word.

First Reading
Responsorial Psalm
Second Reading
Acclamation
Gospel

Homily

Profession of Faith (Nicene Creed)

Prayers of the Faithful

LITURGY OF THE EUCHARIST

During the Liturgy of the Eucharist, we focus on **loving** God.

Offertory (Presentation and Preparation of the Gifts)

Prayer Over the Offerings

<u>The Eucharistic Prayer</u>
Preface • Holy (Sanctus) • The Mystery of Faith (Memorial Acclamation) • Doxology

<u>The Communion Rite</u>
The Lord's Prayer • Sign of Peace • Lamb of God • Communion

The Eucharist is the Sacrament of Love; It signifies Love, It produces Love. – *St. Thomas Aquinas*

Behold the Lamb of God,
behold him who takes away the sins of the world.
Blessed are those called to the supper of the Lamb.

**Lord, I am not worthy
that you should enter under my roof,
but only say the word
and my soul shall be healed.**

Prayer Before the Crucifix

Behold, O kind and gentle Jesus,
I kneel before you and pray
that you would impress upon my heart
the virtues of faith, hope and charity,
with true repentance for my sins
and a firm purpose of amendment.
At the same time, with sorrow
I meditate on your five precious wounds,
having in mind the words which David spoke in prophecy:
"They have pierced my hands and my feet.
I can count all my bones." (Psalm 22)

The Jesus Prayer

Lord Jesus Christ, Son of the living God,
have mercy on me, a sinner.

From the cross, Christ teaches us to love even those who do not love us. - *Pope Francis*

EUCHARISTIC ADORATION

Shortly before Jesus was arrested in the Garden of Gethsemane, He asked His apostles to spend one hour in prayer with Him.

When we make a Holy Hour before the Eucharist, we are in the Real Presence of our Lord. As we pray in the presence of the Blessed Sacrament, we come to know Him, love Him, and worship Him more deeply in the silence of our heart.

Anima Christi

Soul of Christ, sanctify me;
Body of Christ, save me;
Blood of Christ, inebriate me;
Water from the side of Christ, wash me;
Passion of Christ, strengthen me;
O good Jesus, hear me;
Within your wounds hide me;
Separated from you, let me never be;
From the evil one protect me;
At the hour of my death, call me;
And close to you bid me;
That with your saints,
I may be praising you forever and ever. Amen.

The Divine Praises

Blessed be God.
Blessed be His holy name.
Blessed be Jesus Christ, true God and true man.
Blessed be the name of Jesus.
Blessed be His most Sacred Heart.
Blessed be His most precious Blood.
Blessed be Jesus in the Most Holy Sacrament of the Altar.
Blessed be the Holy Spirit, the Paraclete.
Blessed be the great Mother of God, Mary most holy.
Blessed be her holy and Immaculate Conception.
Blessed be her glorious Assumption.
Blessed be the name of Mary, Virgin and Mother.
Blessed be Saint Joseph, her most chaste spouse.
Blessed be God in His angels and in His Saints.

You may be sure that of all the moments of your life, the time you spend before the divine Sacrament will be that which will give you more strength during life and more consolation at the hour of your death and during eternity. - *St. Alphonsus*

THE HOLY ROSARY

The Rosary prayer is a repetitive, Scripture-based devotion in honor of the Virgin Mary that helps us remember, honor, and meditate on the important events in the lives of Jesus and His Blessed Mother.

"Pray the Rosary every day
to obtain peace for the world."
– *Our Lady of Fátima*

OUR LADY OF FATIMA

On May 13, 1917, Our Lady of Fátima appeared to three young children in Fátima, Portugal and asked them to do three things... pray the rosary, do penance (avoid and confess sins), and honor the Immaculate Heart of Mary.

On May 13, 1981, St. Pope John Paul II survived an assassination attempt in St. Peter's Square and credited the Blessed Virgin Mary with saving his life on her feast day. The Feast Day of Our Lady of Fátima is May 13.

Recite your Rosary with faith, with humility, with confidence, and with perseverance. – *St. Louis de Montfort*

THE MYSTERIES OF THE ROSARY

The Glorious Mysteries

1. The Resurrection
2. The Ascension
3. The Descent of the Holy Spirit
4. The Assumption of Mary
5. The Coronation of the Virgin

The Joyful Mysteries

1. The Annunciation
2. The Visitation
3. The Nativity
4. The Presentation of Jesus at the Temple
5. The Finding of Jesus in the Temple

The Sorrowful Mysteries

1. The Agony in the Garden
2. The Scourging at the Pillar
3. The Crowning with Thorns
4. The Carrying of the Cross
5. The Crucifixion

The Luminous Mysteries

1. The Baptism of Jesus in the Jordan
2. The Wedding at Cana
3. Jesus' Proclamation of the Kingdom of God
4. The Transfiguration
5. The Institution of the Eucharist

Pray and mediate on the following mysteries on the following days...

SUNDAY	MONDAY	TUESDAY	WEDNESDAY	THURSDAY	FRIDAY	SATURDAY
Glorious Mysteries	Joyful Mysteries	Sorrowful Mysteries	Glorious Mysteries	Luminous Mysteries	Sorrowful Mysteries	Joyful Mysteries

Sign of the Cross

In the name of the Father, and of the Son
and of the Holy Spirit. Amen.

Apostles' Creed

I believe in God, the Father almighty,
Creator of heaven and earth,
and in Jesus Christ, his only Son, our Lord,
who was conceived by the Holy Spirit,
born of the Virgin Mary,
suffered under Pontius Pilate,
was crucified, died and was buried;
he descended into hell;
on the third day he rose again from the dead;
he ascended into heaven,
and is seated at the right hand of God the Father almighty;
from there he will come to judge the living and the dead.

I believe in the Holy Spirit,
the holy catholic Church,
the communion of saints,
the forgiveness of sins,
the resurrection of the body,
and life everlasting.
Amen.

Hail Mary

Hail Mary, full of Grace,
the Lord is with thee.
Blessed are thou among women,
and blessed is the fruit of thy womb, Jesus.
Holy Mary, Mother of God,
pray for us sinners,
now and at the hour of our death. Amen.

Glory Be

Glory be to the Father,
and to the Son,
and to the Holy Spirit,
as it was in the beginning,
is now, and ever shall be,
world without end. Amen.

Our Father

Our Father, who art in Heaven,
hallowed be Thy name;
Thy kingdom come;
Thy will be done on earth as it is in heaven.
Give us this day our daily bread;
and forgive us our trespasses
as we forgive those who trespass against us;
and lead us not into temptation, but deliver us from evil. Amen.

HOW TO PRAY THE ROSARY

1. Begin with the Sign of the Cross,
   and holding the Crucifix, pray the Apostles' Creed.

2. Pray the Our Father.

3. Pray three Hail Marys (for the virtues of Faith, Hope, and Charity).

4. Pray the Glory Be, announce and meditate on the first mystery,
   then pray the Our Father.

5. Pray ten Hail Marys (called a 'decade').

6. Pray the Glory Be and the Fatima Prayer.

7. Before each of the remaining four decades,
   announce and meditate on the next mystery,
   and then pray the Our Father.

8. After praying the five decades,
   pray the Hail, Holy Queen
   and the concluding Rosary Prayer.

Fatima Prayer

O my Jesus, forgive us our sins, save us from the fires of hell,
and lead all souls to Heaven, especially those in most need of your Mercy.   Amen.

Hail, Holy Queen

Hail, Holy Queen,
Mother of mercy,
our life, our sweetness and our hope.
To thee do we cry,
poor banished children of Eve;
to thee do we send up our sighs,
mourning and weeping
in this vale of tears.
Turn then, most gracious Advocate,
thine eyes of mercy toward us,
and after this our exile,
show unto us
the blessed fruit of thy womb, Jesus,
O clement, O loving,
O sweet Virgin Mary!

V. Pray for us, O holy Mother of God.
R. That we may be made worthy
    of the promises of Christ. Amen.

Rosary Prayer

Let us Pray:
O God, whose only begotten Son,
by his life, death, and resurrection,
has purchased for us
the rewards of eternal life,
grant, we beseech thee,
that while meditating on these mysteries
of the most Holy Rosary
of the Blessed Virgin Mary,
we may imitate what they contain
and obtain what they promise,
through the same Christ our Lord. Amen.

PROMISES OF THE ROSARY

Approximately eight hundred years ago, Our Lady appeared to Saint Dominic and Blessed Alan de la Roche and told them that everyone who faithfully prays the Rosary will receive the following fifteen promises...

1. To all those who shall pray my Rosary devoutly, I promise my special protection and great graces.

2. Those who shall persevere in the recitation of my Rosary will receive some special grace.

3. The Rosary will be a very powerful armor against hell; it will destroy vice, deliver from sin and dispel heresy.

4. The Rosary will make virtue and good works flourish, and will obtain for souls the most abundant divine mercies. It will draw the hearts of men from the love of the world and its vanities, and will lift them to the desire of eternal things. Oh, that souls would sanctify themselves by this means.

5. Those who trust themselves to me through the Rosary will not perish.

6. Whoever recites my Rosary devoutly reflecting on the mysteries, shall never be overwhelmed by misfortune. He will not experience the anger of God nor will he perish by an unprovided death. The sinner will be converted; the just will persevere in grace and merit eternal life.

7. Those truly devoted to my Rosary shall not die without the sacraments of the Church.

8. Those who are faithful to recite my Rosary shall have during their life and at their death the light of God and the plenitude of His graces and will share in the merits of the blessed.

9. I will deliver promptly from purgatory souls devoted to my Rosary.

10. True children of my Rosary will enjoy great glory in heaven.

11. What you shall ask through my Rosary you shall obtain.

12. To those who propagate my Rosary I promise aid in all their necessities.

13. I have obtained from my Son that all the members of the Rosary Confraternity shall have as their intercessors, in life and in death, the entire celestial court.

14. Those who recite my Rosary faithfully are my beloved children, the brothers and sisters of Jesus Christ.

15. Devotion to my Rosary is a special sign of predestination.

The Memorare

Remember, O most gracious Virgin Mary,
that never was it known that anyone who fled to your protection,
implored your help, or sought your intercession, was left unaided.

Inspired by this confidence, I fly unto you,
O Virgin of virgins, my Mother.
To you I come; before you I stand sinful and sorrowful.

O Mother of the Word Incarnate!
Despise not my petitions,
but in your mercy hear and answer me. Amen.

We celebrate the Feast of Our Lady of the Rosary on October 7.

Love our Lady. And she will obtain abundant grace to help you conquer in your daily struggle.
– St. Josemaria Escriva

The Divine Shepherd

The LORD is my Shepherd, I shall not want.
He makes me lie down in green pastures;
He leads me beside still waters;
He restores my soul.
He leads me in right paths
For His Name's sake.

Even though I walk through the darkest valley,
I fear no evil;
For you are with me;
Your rod and Your staff-
they comfort me.

You prepare a table before me
in the presence of my enemies,
You anoint my head with oil;
My cup overflows.
Surely goodness and mercy shall follow me
All the days of my life.
And I shall dwell in the house of the LORD
My whole life long.

Psalm 23:1-6 (NRSV)

The Ten Commandments

1. I am the LORD your God: you shall not have strange Gods before me.

2. You shall not take the name of the LORD your God in vain.

3. Remember to keep holy the LORD'S Day.

4. Honor your father and your mother.

5. You shall not kill.

6. You shall not commit adultery.

7. You shall not steal.

8. You shall not bear false witness against your neighbor.

9. You shall not covet your neighbor's wife.

10. You shall not covet your neighbor's goods.

The Beatitudes
(Sermon on the Mount)

When Jesus saw the crowds, he went up the mountain;
and after he sat down, his disciples came to him.
Then he began to speak, and taught them, saying:

Blessed are the poor in spirit, for theirs is the kingdom of heaven.
Blessed are those who mourn, for they will be comforted.
Blessed are the meek, for they will inherit the earth.
Blessed are those who hunger and thirst for righteousness, for they will be filled.
Blessed are the merciful, for they will receive mercy.
Blessed are the pure in heart, for they will see God.
Blessed are the peacemakers, for they will be called children of God.
Blessed are those who are persecuted for righteousness' sake, for theirs is the kingdom of heaven.

Blessed are you when people revile you and persecute you and utter all kinds of evil against you falsely on my account.

Rejoice and be glad, for your reward is great in heaven, for in the same way they persecuted the prophets who were before you.

Matthew 5:1-12 (NRSV)

THE COMMUNION OF SAINTS

As Catholics, we gather together in communion with God and each other to celebrate our faith.
Our relationship with the Lord is not just about 'God and me', but rather 'God and we'.

In our Catholic tradition of community and fellowship, we also call upon the saints to bring us closer to God
and to help us in our times of need. We call these prayers the Intercession of Saints.

If you live a life of holiness, you too can become a saint.

What does it mean to live a life of holiness?

You live a holy life one moment at a time
by becoming the person God made you to be.

When God created you, He gave you special talents
and a unique personality so you could follow His plan for your life.

God doesn't want you to be someone you're not.
God simply wants you to be the special person He created you to be.

If you are what you should be, you will set the whole world on fire. - *St. Catherine of Siena*

WHAT IS THE PROCESS FOR BECOMING A SAINT?

The 4 steps for becoming a saint are...

1. NOMINATION

Typically a bishop begins someone's 'cause for sainthood' a number of years after their death by investigating their virtuous life. The person is now called "**Servant of God**".

2. DETERMINATION

The *Congregation for the Causes of the Saints* then recommends the Pope declare that the candidate lived a 'life of heroic virtue'. The person is now called "**Venerable**".

3. BEATIFICATION

If the candidate is not a martyr, there needs to be proof that the candidate responded to prayers and interceded by performing a miracle. The person is now called "**Blessed**".

4. CANONIZATION

The candidate needs to intercede again and perform a second miracle. The person is called "**Saint**" and is assigned a feast day.

"God Love You."

Archbishop Fulton Sheen was born in 1895 and grew up in Peoria, Illinois. He wrote 73 books and hosted a popular Emmy-winning TV show called "Life is Worth Living".

He later became Bishop of the Diocese of Rochester, New York and titular Archbishop of Wales. Archbishop Sheen died in 1979 in New York and was interred in St. Patrick's Cathedral.

Venerable Archbishop Fulton J. Sheen is currently in the process of the *Cause for Canonization*.

Venerable Archbishop Fulton J. Sheen

RECENTLY CANONIZED SAINTS

St. Padre Pio was a mystic and priest
with the Order of Capuchin Friars Minor in Italy.
He received the stigmata when he was 31,
and lived under constant scrutiny
until his death because of these visible wounds
of our crucified Lord and Savior.

Pray, hope, and don't worry. – *St. Padre Pio*

PADRE PIO

St. Kateri Tekakwitha, the "Lily of the Mohawks",
was a Native American from Canada
who converted to Catholicism as a teenager.
Despite being persecuted for her conversion,
she remained devoted to her faith and chastity.

Jesus, I love you. – *St. Kateri Tekakwitha*

KATERI TEKAKWITHA

St. Josephine Bakhita was born in Sudan, Africa. As a young girl she was taken from her home and forced to become a slave. She was able to escape slavery when she joined the Canossian Sisters in Venice, Italy.

I am definitely loved and whatever happens to me, I am awaited by this love. And so my life is good. *-St. Josephine Bakhita*

JOSEPHINE BAKHITA

St. John Paul II, the first Pope from Poland, served as Pontiff for nearly 27 years. He was devoted to uniting people from all faiths as he visited 129 countries while also influencing political leaders throughout the world.

Be not afraid. – *St. John Paul II*

POPE JOHN PAUL II

Novena Prayer to St. Thomas Aquinas

St. Thomas Aquinas,
patron of students and Catholic schools,
I thank God for the gifts of light and knowledge
he bestowed on you, which you used to build up
the Church in love.
I thank God, too, for the wealth and richness
of theological teaching you left in your writings.

Not only were you a great teacher,
you lived a life of virtue and you made holiness
the desire of your heart.

If I cannot imitate you in the brilliance
of your academic pursuits, I can follow you
in the humility and charity which marked your life.
As St. Paul said, charity is the greatest gift,
and it is open to all.

Pray for me that I might grow in holiness and charity.
Pray also for Catholic schools, and for all students.
In particular, please obtain the favor I ask
during this novena (mention your request). Amen.

Prayer of St. Thomas Aquinas

Grant, O Merciful God,
that I may ardently desire,
prudently examine,
truthfully acknowledge
and perfectly accomplish
what is pleasing to you,
for the praise and glory
of your name. Amen.

The child grew and became strong, filled with wisdom; and the favor of God was upon him.
Luke 2:40 (NRSV)

St. Francis of Assisi
Feast Day: October 4

Prayer of St. Francis of Assisi

Lord, make me an instrument of Your peace.
Where there is hatred, let me sow love;
where there is injury, pardon;
where there is doubt, faith;
where there is despair, hope;
where there is darkness, light;
and where there is sadness, joy.

O, Divine Master, grant that I may not so much seek
to be consoled, as to console;
to be understood, as to understand;
to be loved, as to love;
For it is in giving that we receive;
it is in pardoning that we are pardoned;
and it is in dying that we are born to eternal life.

If you want peace, work for justice. - *Bl. Pope Paul VI*

St. Jude Thaddeus
Feast Day: October 28

A Prayer to St. Jude for Today

St. Jude, may your path of hope be mine in the days ahead.
I promise in faith to share your hope with others,
to forgive as I am forgiven by my Father in heaven,
and to show caring and kindness at every opportunity.

Guide me, St. Jude, so that I begin each new day
with gratitude, truth, and hope in my heart.

Challenge me, St. Jude, to end each day
reflecting on my actions and motivations
so that I grow in faith, love, and hope. Amen.

A Prayer to St. Jude for Hope

God the Father, give me hope.
Help me to know that your hope is alive in me
as I offer kindness, forgiveness, and tenderness to others.
I seek the calm that comes from trusting
in your hope and your healing presence.

I trust that your servant St. Jude walks with me
in all the blessings and challenges of my life,
and intercedes on behalf of my petitions.

St. Jude, fill my heart with hope. Amen.

Serenity Prayer

God, grant me the serenity to accept the things I cannot change,
courage to change the things I can change,
and the wisdom to know the difference.

- Reinhold Niebuhr

For surely I know the plans I have for you, says the LORD, plans for your welfare and not for harm,
to give you a future with hope. – *Jeremiah 29:11 (NRSV)*

St. John Vianney
Feast Day: August 4

We often ask priests to pray for us and our loved ones. While they pray for us, let us remember to pray for them.

Prayer for Priests

O Jesus, I pray for Your faithful and fervent priests;
for Your unfaithful and tepid priests;
for Your priests laboring at home,
or abroad in distant mission fields;
for Your tempted priests;
for Your lonely and desolate priests;
for Your young priests;
for Your dying priests;
for the souls of Your priests in purgatory.

Above all I recommend to You
the priests dearest to me;
the priest who baptized me;
the priests who absolved me from my sins;
the priests at whose Masses I assisted and
who gave me Your Body and Blood in Holy Communion;
the priests who taught and instructed me;
all the priests to whom I am indebted in any other way.
O Jesus, keep them all close to your heart,
and bless them abundantly in time and in eternity. Amen.

Prayer for Vocations

Father you call each one of us by name
and ask us to follow you.

Bless your church by raising up
dedicated and generous leaders
from our families and friends
who will serve your people
as Sisters, Priests, Brothers,
Deacons, and Lay Ministers.

Inspire us as we grow to know you,
and open our hearts to hear your call.

We ask this in Jesus name. Amen.

The priesthood is the love of the heart of Jesus. – *St. John Vianney*

St. Ignatius of Loyola
Feast Day: July 31

Ad majorem Dei gloriam.
To the greater glory of God.

Suscipe

Take, Lord, and receive all my liberty,
my memory, my understanding
and my entire will,
All I have and call my own.

You have given all to me.
To you, Lord, I return it.

Everything is yours; do with it what you will.
Give me only your love and your grace.
That is enough for me.

- St. Ignatius of Loyola

It's not hard to obey when we love the one whom we obey. - *St. Ignatius of Loyola*

St. Thérèse of Lisieux
(The Little Flower)

Feast Day: October 1

Prayer to St. Thérèse of Lisieux

O Little Thérèse of the Child Jesus,
please pick a rose for me from the heavenly gardens
and send it to me as a message of love.

O Little Flower of Jesus,
ask God today to grant the favors
I now place with confidence in your hands.

(mention your specific requests)

St. Thérèse,
help me to always believe,
 as you did,
in God's great love for me,
so that I might imitate your "Little Way" each day. Amen.

We celebrate the feast of
Our Lady of Mount Carmel on July 16.

**The Scapular of
Our Lady of Mount Carmel**
(Brown Scapular)

"Take this Scapular,
it shall be a sign of salvation,
a protection in danger
and a pledge of peace.
Whosoever dies wearing this Scapular
shall not suffer eternal fire."

– Spoken by Our Lady of Mount Carmel
to St. Simon Stock

Miss no single opportunity of making some small sacrifice, here by a smiling look, there by a kindly word;
always doing the smallest right and doing it all for love. - St. Thérèse of Lisieux

St. Patrick
Feast Day: March 17

St. Patrick Breastplate

Christ be with me, Christ within me
Christ behind me, Christ before me
Christ beside me, Christ to win me
Christ to comfort me and restore me.
Christ beneath me, Christ above me
Christ in quiet, Christ in danger
Christ in hearts of all that love me
Christ in mouth of friend or stranger.

An Irish Blessing

May the road rise to meet you,
May the wind be always at your back,
May the sun shine warm upon your face,
The rains fall soft upon your fields and,
Until we meet again,
May God hold you in the palm of His hand.

I am imperfect in many things, nevertheless I want my brethren and kinsfolk to know my nature so that they may be able to perceive my soul's desire. – *St. Patrick*

St. Cecilia
Feast Day: November 22

The Musician's Prayer

Oh Lord, please bless this music
that it might glorify your name.
May the talent that you have bestowed upon me
be used only to serve you.

Let this music be a witness to your majesty and love,
and remind us that you are always watching,
and listening, from your throne above.

May your presence and beauty be found in every note,
and may the words that are sung reach the hearts
of your people so they will draw closer to you.

May your Spirit guide us through every measure
so that we might be the instruments of your peace,
and proclaim your glory with glad voices. Amen.

I will sing to the LORD as long as I live; I will sing praise to my God while I have being.
Psalm 104: 33 (NRSV)

St. Norbert
Feast Day: June 6

Prayer of St. Norbert

Father,
you made the Bishop Norbert
an outstanding minister of your Church,
renowned for his preaching and pastoral zeal.
Always grant to your Church faithful shepherds
to lead your people to eternal salvation.

Through our Lord Jesus Christ, your Son,
who lives and reigns with you
in the unity of the Holy Spirit,
one God, forever and ever. Amen.

- Collect Prayer at Mass

Faith is to believe what you do not see; the reward of this faith is to see what you believe. – *St. Augustine*

THE DIVINE MERCY

The Divine Mercy message and devotion focuses on the infinite mercy that God shows to us and wants us to show to others.

Maria Faustina Kowalska, a Polish sister of the Congregation of the Sisters of Our Lady of Mercy, wrote about the apparitions and conversations she had with Jesus about His mercy in a *Diary: Divine Mercy in My Soul*.

In these visits, Jesus told St. Faustina "Proclaim that Mercy is the greatest attribute of God. Every soul believing and trusting in My Mercy will obtain it." He also taught her how to pray the Divine Mercy Chaplet.

Divine Mercy Sunday is celebrated on the Second Sunday of Easter.

DIVINE MERCY CHAPLET

The three reasons for praying the Divine Mercy Chaplet are to obtain mercy, to trust in God's mercy, and to show mercy for others.

The most meaningful time to pray this Chaplet is at 3 p.m., the Hour of Mercy.

Using the beads on the Rosary, we pray the Divine Mercy Chaplet as follows...

1. Begin with the **Sign of the Cross**, one **Our Father,** one **Hail Mary**, and **The Apostles' Creed**.

2. On each large bead, pray…
   Eternal Father, I offer You the Body and Blood, Soul and Divinity of Your dearly beloved Son, Our Lord Jesus Christ, in atonement for our sins and those of the whole world.

3. On each of the small beads, pray…
   For the sake of His sorrowful Passion, have mercy on us and on the whole world.

4. Repeat steps 2 and 3 for the remaining four decades.

5. Conclude by praying the following prayer *three times*…
   Holy God, Holy Mighty One, Holy Immortal One, have mercy on us and on the whole world.

Words of Our Lady of Guadalupe to Juan Diego

Know for certain, least of my sons,
that I am the perfect and perpetual Virgin Mary,
Mother of the True God through whom everything lives,
the Lord of all things near and far,
the Master of heaven and earth.

It is my earnest wish that a temple be built here to my honor.
Here I will demonstrate, I will exhibit,
I will give all my love, my compassion, my help and my protection to the people.

I am your merciful mother,
the merciful mother of all of you who live united in this land, and of all mankind,
of all those who love me, of those who cry to me, of those who seek me,
of those who have confidence in me.

Here I will hear their weeping, their sorrow,
and will remedy and alleviate all their multiple sufferings, necessities and misfortunes.

As God's chosen ones, holy beloved, clothe yourselves with compassion,
kindness, humility, meekness, and patience. *Colossians 3:12 (NRSV)*

St. Michael the Archangel
Feast Day: September 29

Prayer to St. Michael

St. Michael the Archangel, defend us in battle.
Be our defense against the wickedness
and snares of the Devil.
May God rebuke him,
we humbly pray, and do thou,
O Prince of the heavenly hosts,
by the power of God, thrust into hell Satan,
and all the evil spirits, who prowl about the
world seeking the ruin of souls. Amen.

- Pope Leo XIII

Prayer for the Safety of a Solider

Almighty and eternal God,
those who take refuge in you will be glad
and forever will shout for joy.
Protect these soldiers
as they discharge their duties.
Protect them with the shield of your strength
and keep them safe from all evil and harm.
May the power of your love enable them
to return home in safety,
that with all who love them,
they may ever praise you for your loving care.
We ask this through Christ our Lord. Amen.

Do not be overcome by evil, but overcome evil with good. *Romans 12:21 (NRSV)*

St. Anthony
Feast Day: June 13

Prayer to Find What is Lost

Dear St. Anthony,
you are the patron of the poor and the helper of all who seek lost articles.
Help me to find what I have lost, (mention what you have lost)
so that I will be able to make better use of the time that I will gain
for God's greater honor and glory.

Grant your gracious aid to all people who seek what they have lost,
especially those who seek to regain God's grace. Amen.

Ask, and it will be given you; search, and you will find; knock, and the door will be opened for you.
Matthew 7:7 (NRSV)

St. Christopher

Prayer to St. Christopher (The Motorist's Prayer)

Protect me today in all my travels
along the road's way.
Give your warning sign if danger is near
so that I may stop while the path is clear.
Be at my window and direct me through
when the vision blurs From out of the blue
Carry me safely to my destined place,
like you carried Christ in your close
embrace. Amen.

Prayer Before Starting on a Journey

My holy Angel Guardian,
ask the Lord to bless the journey
which I undertake, that it may profit the health
of my soul and body;
that I may reach its end, and that,
returning safe and sound,
I may find my family in good health.

I am going to send an angel in front of you,
to guard you on the way and to bring you to the place that I have prepared. *Exodus 23:20 (NRSV)*

Your Guardian Angel
Feast Day: October 2

Guardian Angel Prayer
(Morning Prayer)

Angel of God,
My Guardian Dear,
to whom His love commits me here,
ever this day be at my side,
to light and to guard,
to rule and guide. Amen.

Good Night My Guardian Angel
(Evening Prayer)

Good night, my Guardian Angel,
The day has sped away;
Well spent or ill,
its story Is written down for aye.
And now, of God's kind Providence,
Thou image pure and bright,
Watch over me while I'm sleeping.
My Angel dear, good night!

Morning Offering

O Jesus, through the Immaculate Heart of Mary,
I offer you my prayers, works, joys, and sufferings of this day
for all the intentions of your Sacred Heart,
in union with the Holy Sacrifice of the Mass throughout the world,
for the salvation of souls, the reparation of sins, the reunion of all Christians,
and in particular for the intentions of the Holy Father this month. Amen.

Remember that you have an angel as a companion, guardian, and friend. - *St. John Bosco*

The Holy Family
Feast Day: First Sunday after Christmas

Prayer to the Holy Family

Jesus, Son of God and Son of Mary, bless our family.
Graciously inspire in us the unity, peace and mutual love
that you found in your own family
in the little town of Nazareth.

Mary, Mother of Jesus and our Mother,
nourish our family with your faith and your love.
Keep us close to your Son, Jesus, in all our sorrows and joys.

Joseph, Foster-father to Jesus, guardian and spouse of Mary,
keep our family safe from harm.
Help us in all times of discouragement or anxiety.

Holy Family of Nazareth, make our family one with you.
Help us to be instruments of peace.
Grant that love, strengthened by grace,
may prove mightier than all the weaknesses and trials
through which our families sometimes pass.
May we always have God at the center
of our hearts and homes until we are all one family,
happy and at peace in our true home with you. Amen.

Parent's Prayer

All praise to you, Lord Jesus, Lover of children;
Bless our family and help us to lead our children to You.

Give us light, strength, and courage
when our task is difficult.
Let your spirit fill us with love and peace,
So that we may help our children to love you.

All glory and praise are yours, Lord Jesus, for ever and ever.
Amen.

If I had to advise parents, I should tell them to take great care about the people with whom their children associate...
Much harm may result from bad company, and we are inclined by nature
to follow what is worse than what is better. – *St. Elizabeth Ann Seton*

Footprints

One night I had a dream...

I dreamed I was walking along the beach with the Lord,
and across the sky flashed scenes from my life.
For each scene I noticed two sets of footprints in the sand;
One belonged to me, and the other to the Lord.
When the last scene of my life flashed before us,
I looked back at the footprints in the sand.
I noticed that many times along the path of my life,
there was only one set of footprints.

I also noticed that it happened at the very lowest and saddest times in my life.
This really bothered me, and I questioned the Lord about it.
"Lord, you said that once I decided to follow you,
You would walk with me all the way;
But I have noticed that during the most troublesome times in my life,
there is only one set of footprints.
I don't understand why in times when I needed you the most,
you should leave me."

The Lord replied, "My precious, precious child.
I love you, and I would never, never leave you
during your times of trial and suffering.
When you saw only one set of footprints,
It was then that I carried you."

When I am afraid, I put my trust in you. *Psalm 56:3 (NRSV)*

A New Heart

Give me a heart of courage, that I may follow Thee,
a heart of joy, that I may sing with Thee,
a heart of praise, that I may adore Thee,
a heart of gratitude, that I may thank Thee,
a heart of kindness, that I may emulate Thee,
a heart of hospitality, that I may welcome Thee,
a heart of hope, that I may trust in Thee.
a heart of compassion, that I may cry with Thee.
a heart of simplicity, that I may walk with Thee.
a gentle heart, that I may imitate Thee.
a missionary heart, that I may go with Thee.

- Robert F. Morneau

A new heart I will give you, and a new spirit I will put within you; and I will remove from your body
the heart of stone and give you a heart of flesh. *Ezekiel 36:26 (NRSV)*

The Road Ahead

My Lord God, I have no idea where I am going.
I do not see the road ahead of me.
I cannot know for certain where it will end.
Nor do I really know myself,
and the fact that I think that I am following
your will does not mean that I am actually doing so.
But I believe that the desire to please you
does in fact please you.
And I hope I have that desire in all that I am doing.
I hope that I will never do anything apart from that desire.
And I know that if I do this you will lead me
by the right road though I may know nothing about it.
Therefore will I trust you always
though I may seem to be lost and in the shadow of death.
I will not fear, for you are ever with me,
and you will never leave me to face my perils alone.

- Thomas Merton

The Road of Life

I expect to pass through this world but once.
Any good, therefore, that I can do
or any kindness I can show to any fellow creature,
let me do it now... for I shall not pass this way again.

Love God, serve God; everything is in that. - *St. Clare of Assisi*

Go in peace, glorifying the Lord by your life.

Thanks be to God.